For Simone,
with my love
Great-Grandma C.
1988

Earthworms, Dirt, and Rotten Leaves

AN EXPLORATION IN ECOLOGY

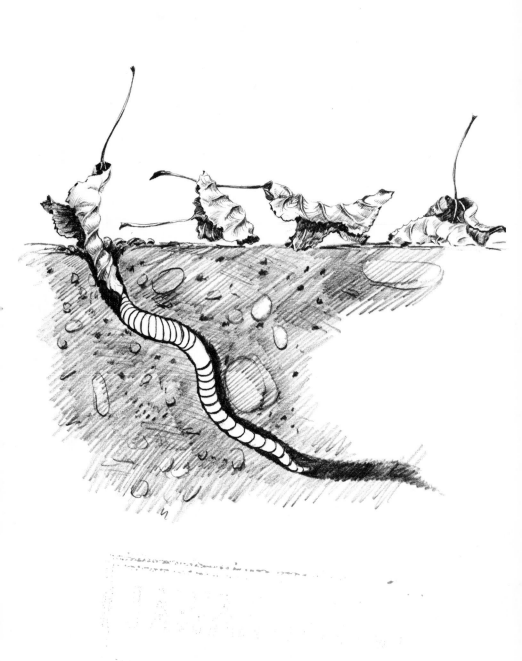

Earthworms, Dirt, and Rotten Leaves

AN EXPLORATION IN ECOLOGY

by Molly McLaughlin

illustrated by Robert Shetterly

ATHENEUM 🦫 NEW YORK

Text copyright © 1986 by Molly McLaughlin
Illustrations copyright © 1986 by Robert Shetterly

Atheneum
Macmillan Publishing Company
866 Third Avenue, New York, NY 10022

Type set by Graphic Composition, Athens, Georgia
Printed & bound by Fairfield Graphics, Inc. Fairfield, Pennsylvania
Designed by Marilyn Marcus

10 9 8 7 6 5 4 3 2

Library of Congress Cataloging in Publication Data

McLaughlin, Molly.
    Earthworms, dirt, and rotten leaves.

    Bibliography: p. 82
    Includes index.
    Summary: Examines the earthworm and its environment,
suggesting experiments to introduce basic ecological
concepts as demonstrated by the earthworm's survival in
its habitat.
    1. Earthworms—Juvenile literature. 2. Soil ecology—
Juvenile literature. [1. Earthworms. 2. Soil ecology.
3. Ecology] I. Title.
QL391.M38   1986   595.1'46045   86-3318
ISBN 0-689-31215-6

FOR

Bud and Colin

Contents

CHAPTER 1

Why Worms?

Why would anyone want to have anything to do with earthworms? They're not very big, and they're certainly not pretty. They live in the dirt and eat dead leaves.

But, in fact, their home and their habits and their not-too-charming appearance are exactly what make earthworms a lot more interesting than you might expect.

First of all, earthworms are a wonderful, streamlined example of how living things become adapted, or suited, to their environment. If you had to think up an animal especially designed to live underground and eat leaves, it would be hard to come up with anything better.

Second, the earthworm is a small animal that has a huge effect on its home environment. Earthworms make tunnels in the soil and mix up its different layers, they pull leaves under and bring topsoil up, they add fertilizer and move stones.

Now the soil that's home to earthworms is also the residence of billions of other animals, and it's the place where plants grow. Since all animals, including humans, depend on plants for food, the soil is more than just dirt to us as well. It's at the very foundation of our food supply. And at the foundation of the most fertile and productive soil of all, there is the earthworm, whose activities make soil conditions more favorable for plant growth.

Third, as the earthworms go about their business eating old rotten leaves, they take part in one of the most important processes on our planet: the *recycling*, or reusing, of the basic chemical materials that plants and animals need to live and grow.

All living things are involved in this recycling — we all use "stuff" that's previously been part of something else. But earthworms, like many even smaller and less-charming organisms, are involved in a really essential part of recycling called *decomposition*. Decomposition is what happens when the materials in the bodies of dead plants and animals are broken down into the simpler parts that can be used again by new organisms.

If this process of decay or decomposition didn't go on, the basic chemicals of life would stay locked up in the bodies of dead plants and animals forever,

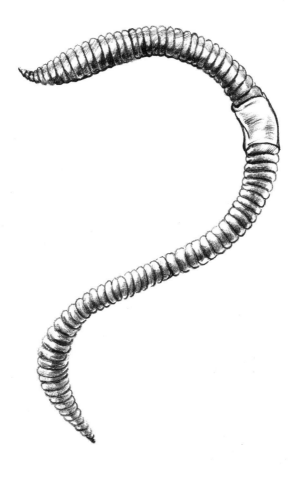

What's so interesting about a slimy creature that lives in the dirt and eats dead leaves?

and eventually all the supplies would be used up and no new plants or animals could grow. So we all depend on *decomposers,* including earthworms, to keep us from running out of essential supplies.

Finding out more about this slimy, squirmy, but surprisingly important creature is the aim of this book. We will pay a lot of attention to how the worm looks and how it acts, but also to its home and its neighbors and how it fits in with them. After all, the earthworm doesn't exist in the world all by itself. Like every other living creature, it's part of a community of plants and animals, all connected with each other as they go about making a living in their particular environments. Finding out how the earthworm fits into its community will help you understand how other animals fit into their own special situations as well.

It's possible to read the book straight through; or you can use it like a guidebook and try the activities as you go along. Doing these experiments and making observations yourself will help you get a firsthand, closeup idea of what the earthworm is like. It will also give you practice in doing some genuine scientific investigation on your own. Making observations, asking questions, comparing notes, and taking guesses are some of the methods that scientists use to find things out, whether in fancy laboratories or in ordinary backyards. Depending on what's being investigated, the equipment used and the location of the research may be quite different, but the processes of investigation are very much like those we will use to study the earthworm and its neighborhood.

A final reason for watching worms is that they're so convenient. It might be more exciting to observe kangaroos or whales or other more rare and exotic animals, but you'd have to make a long trip and have some very special equipment. You can find earthworms almost anywhere. There are lots of them. And they can't possibly hurt you.

So, to begin, find a worm.

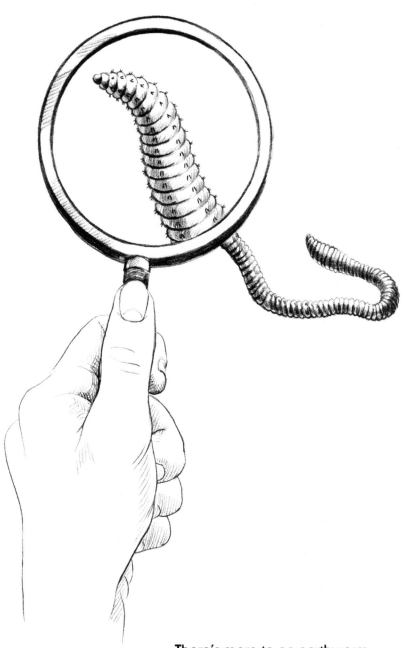

There's more to an earthworm
than at first meets your eye.

CHAPTER 2

A Guide to Watching Worms

Unless you live at the North Pole or in a desert, it probably won't be too hard to find an earthworm and look at it. All you have to do is step outside and dig one up.

But just looking at a worm isn't the same as really looking at one — that is, watching it very carefully, paying close attention, and trying to see things you haven't noticed before. Such careful watching is called *observing*. This guide will give you some suggestions for observing earthworms. It will also help you to *interpret* your observations as you figure out why the things you observe might be important for the earthworm and its life underground.

The only equipment you really need for worm watching is a shovel or trowel for digging. You might also want paper for writing or drawing; and although you can see plenty with your own eyes, a magnifying glass will help you get a closer look.

Start by drawing a picture of an earthworm, putting in all the details you can remember. Or, think about how you might describe an earthworm to someone who had never seen one — a visitor from outer space, for example. This will give you some ideas of what to look for when you begin observing.

It's also a good idea to make a checklist of things that you especially want to notice. Leave some space for writing notes, and use your list as a guide to make sure you don't overlook anything while you've got the worm right there in front of you. The list will also help you remember what you've seen after the worm is out of sight. Later on you can use a similar checklist to observe other animals and then make some comparisons — how the various animals move, for example, or how their body shapes are different.

Here are some suggestions for an earthworm observation guide. Be sure to add any ideas of your own.

Earthworm Observation Guide

1. What shape is the earthworm?
2. What color?
3. How long is it? (How did you measure it?)
4. Does the earthworm have legs? eyes? ears? nose? mouth? stripes?
5. Is there a difference between the top side of the worm and underneath? If there is, what is it?
6. Is there a difference between the front end of the worm and the tail? If there is, what is it?
7. How does the worm's skin feel?
8. Are there any other special features that you notice?
9. How does the worm move?
10. How fast does it go?
11. Does the worm ever move backwards?
12. What happens when the worm meets another worm?
13. What happens when the worm comes to a hole?
14. What does the worm do when it comes to an obstacle like a rock or a big clod of dirt?
15. Do you think the earthworm has a skeleton? Why or why not?
16. How long does it take the worm to burrow under the ground and disappear?
17. Where did you find the worm? Was it under the ground or on top, out in the open or covered up with something?
18. What else was in the vicinity where you found the worm? (Soil, rocks, sand, puddles, insects,

polar bears, other animals, rusty bedsprings, or
what?)

19 What did the worm do when you dug it up or
uncovered it?
20 If you held it in your hand, what did it do then?
21 Surprises: Leave some space to write down observations you didn't think of beforehand, and
questions you forgot to ask.

When your list is ready, the next step is finding
a worm to watch.

With a few exceptions, you can usually find
earthworms fairly easily in most parts of the world. If
the weather is very cold or very dry, the earthworms
burrow down deeper into the ground where the conditions are better. They don't seem to care too much
for soil that's highly *acidic*, as it is in pine forests, or
for the sand at the beach. It may be a little harder to
find worms if you live right in the middle of a big city
where the soil is compacted or covered with concrete.
But they're around, in yards and gardens and parks,
so don't give up.

The best places to look are under piles of old
leaves or compost heaps. If you don't find any worms
right away, look for holes or tunnels that show where
they might have been, or for the small pellets of soil
that they leave behind.

While you're digging, you might accidentally
chop right through a worm that happened to be in
your way. If you do, don't feel too bad. Getting cut in

half by gardeners is just one of the many accidents that can happen to a worm. Earthworms can often grow new sections if they're cut at a certain part of their bodies. But try not to do it on purpose, either. Earthworms do have nerves and are very sensitive; so even if they do grow new parts, getting cut in half probably doesn't feel too good.

Speaking of feeling good, you may be a little squeamish about picking up a worm if you've never done it before. In fact, some people never get used to it. Don't feel that you have to touch the worm if you don't want to. You can see just as much if you pick it up carefully with a shovel, a flat stick like a tongue depressor, or a plastic spoon. That way you won't suddenly change your mind and give the worm a big shock when you drop it. Remember that the worm can't possibly hurt you, but you can hurt it; so always be as careful and as gentle as you can.

When you finally discover a worm, lay it carefully on the ground and settle down to watch. Using your checklist as a guide, notice everything that you can. Make quick notes on your checklist, so that you won't forget any of your observations.

While you're watching, try to figure out how the things you see might help the earthworm to survive in its underground home. Like all living things, earthworms have developed certain unique features that help them to stay alive and make a living in their own special environment, or *habitat*. To survive, earthworms have to be able to get food and water, shelter, and protection from hazards; they need contact with other earthworms and some safety for their young. The specialized characteristics that help them do all these things in their underground habitat are called *adaptations*. Adaptations can be physical characteristics or ways of behaving; and many of the earthworms' survival tools are traits you can actually observe yourself.

If your worm is lying still, the first features you'll notice will probably be its long thin shape and dirtlike color. You may also see a wide whitish band around its body. This *clitellum* means that your worm is an adult and can mate with any other adult worm and lay eggs. Look closely at what seem to be stripes. They are really places where the worm's body is divided into rings, or *segments*. (Animals like this are called *annelids*, which means "ringed.")

If you have found an active earthworm, the most dramatic characteristic is probably the way it moves. Earthworms can bend and squirm, reach up into the air, curl around things, and go forward and backward. (Can you tell which end is which?) They can change shape from longer and thinner to shorter and fatter, and back again.

When the worm is traveling, watch how it stretches out and then pulls its body up, and how it pokes around to investigate obstacles in its path — sticks, clods of dirt, the edge of the hole you dug, or another worm. If it starts to dig under the ground, see if you can tell how it pushes the dirt aside and pulls its body into the burrow. Time it to see how fast it moves and how long it takes to disappear.

Imagine trying to move like this yourself, and think about how the earthworm must be built. An earthworm's movement is made possible by two sets of muscles. One set circles around each ring; and when these muscles squeeze together, they make the worm stretch out and get thinner. The other set of muscles is arranged along the length of the worm, connecting the rings with each other. When the long muscles pull together, the worm becomes shorter and fatter or bends from one side to the other. The alternating action of these two sets of muscles makes the worm move along.

This very flexible motion and the earthworm's streamlined shape are adaptations that help it to push through the soil where it finds its food and other survival necessities.

You can find another feature that helps the worm move if you rub your finger very gently along its sides. Besides soft, moist skin, you may feel something kind of bristly or hairy. Each segment has eight of these tiny bristles, or *setae*. The setae are not legs, but they do provide traction to make it easier for the worm to move along.

To get an idea of how this helps, put the worm on an enameled pan or a plate. Notice how much harder it seems for the worm to move on a smooth surface than over the soil or on a damp paper towel full of rough places to grab onto.

Bristles help the worm to survive in another way as well. They make it a lot harder to pull the worm out of its burrow if it doesn't want to go. If you've

Two sets of muscles help the earthworm move.

CIRCULAR MUSCLES

Contraction of these elongate the worm.

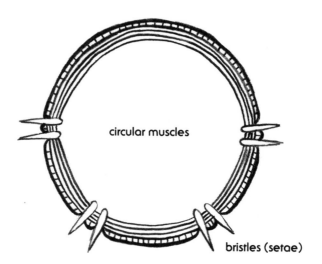

circular muscles

bristles (setae)

When the circular muscles squeeze together or *contract*, the worm gets longer and thinner.

The *setae* or bristles help the worm cling to the sides of the burrow as it moves along.

LONGITUDINAL MUSCLES

Contraction of these shorten and fatten the worm.

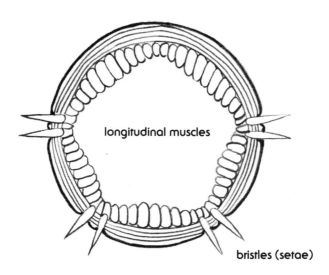

longitudinal muscles

bristles (setae)

Contraction of the long muscles makes the worm shorter and fatter.

ever watched a robin pulling a worm out of the grass, you may have wondered why the bird seemed to be having such a hard time when it's so much bigger and heavier than the worm. To find out for yourself, *gently* try to pull a worm out of the ground after it has decided to go under. Earthworms are a lot stronger than they look!

Another protective adaptation is the earthworm's brownish color. This makes the worm much harder to see against the soil than if it were bright yellow, for example, and therefore helps to protect it from *predators* — animals that would like to eat it. Earthworms are also protected by their habit of staying under the ground except at night. These adaptations help to keep the worm from being eaten by predators that depend on sight; but of course they don't help at all against moles and other predators that live underground and don't need to see.

Earthworms don't need to see either, since they spend most of their time under the ground where it's dark. You won't find any eyes on your worm, but they can tell light from dark and will react to light if it's bright enough, or if it shines on them for a long time. You can test this behavior by shining a bright flashlight on the worm, especially near the front. The worm may wriggle vigorously or try to move away.

You may also notice that the worms won't stay above ground in the sunlight for very long. Avoiding the light helps to keep the worms out of sight of predators; but it also helps them survive by protecting them from getting dried out by the sun. Earthworms

It's not so easy to pull a worm out of its burrow! The bristly setae help it to hang on.

have to stay moist in order to breathe. You won't find a nose on an earthworm, and there are no lungs inside. An earthworm "breathes" when oxygen from the air or water passes right through its damp skin into the blood vessels. Getting dried out is fatal for an earthworm.

Earthworms are the mole's favorite food.

You won't find ears on an earthworm, either, and it seems that they can't really hear sounds that come through the air. They are very sensitive to vibrations that come through the soil, though. In fact, some people who catch worms for fishing bait say that they can make the worms come out of the ground by drumming on it in a certain way.

One theory to explain this is that the worms may leave the ground because the vibrations could mean that a mole is coming. Since moles eat earthworms, getting out of the way would certainly be a useful adaptation.

To test earthworms' sensitivity to sound, Charles Darwin — one of the earliest and most famous earthworm observers — tried playing notes on a whistle. The worms didn't respond at all. But when he put the worms in a flowerpot on the piano and began to play, they got very excited — probably because they could feel the vibrations coming from the piano through the soil in the pot. You might want to try this experiment yourself, to find out if your worms respond the same way.

After you have gotten to know one worm fairly well, try observing another one. Do they seem to be exactly alike, or do you think you might be able to tell them apart?

When your worms have burrowed back under the ground, try drawing another picture. You'll probably find that you know a lot more about earthworms than you did before.

~~~~~~~~~~~~~~~~~~~~~~~~~~~~~~

CHAPTER 3

The Earthworm at Home

To find out more about how earthworms live, the best thing to do would be to watch them going about their usual business in their natural habitat. But you can't do this with earthworms, because they spend most of their time underground.

What you can do is put a few worms in a place that is as much as possible like their usual habitat but that also allows you a view of some of their activities.

A good container for this kind of observation is a clear-sided one that can be filled with dirt deep enough to let the worms dig down at least ten inches. An old fish tank (minus the fish) would be just about right; or you could use a large, one-gallon pickle jar.

But these aren't always easy to find, and the glass could be dangerous if you drop the container — it's going to be very heavy when it's filled with dirt!

An inexpensive container for watching one or two worms is easy to make; and the only special material you need is a piece of clear plastic sheet, called acetate, which you can get at art supply stores and hobby shops. You won't be able to see through the acetate quite as well as you can see through glass, but the acetate is very light, and it won't break.

What You'll Need (Materials) ═══════════════

- Coffee can or tall frozen juice can
- Clear plastic sheet (acetate; get the heaviest you can find)
- Clear tape
- Can opener
- Cheesecloth or screen
- Black paper or aluminum foil
- Rubber band
- Nylon screen, or piece of plastic, cut to fit inside the can (punch some small holes in the plastic for drainage)
- Soil
- Sand or gravel

What to Do (Procedure) ═══════════════════

1 With the can opener, punch a few holes in the bottom of the can for drainage.

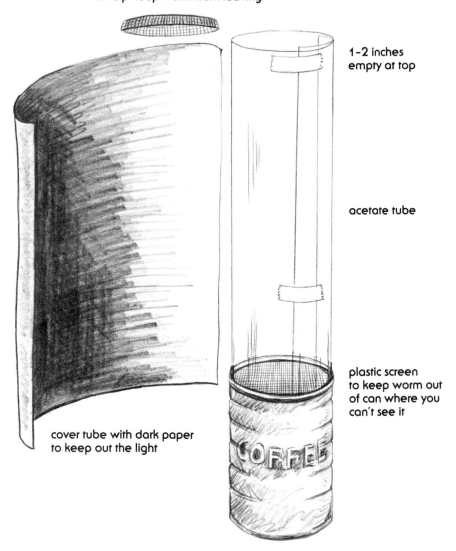

screen or cheesecloth on top
to help keep worm from leaving

1-2 inches
empty at top

acetate tube

plastic screen
to keep worm out
of can where you
can't see it

cover tube with dark paper
to keep out the light

COFFEE

A simple observation container can help you watch
earthworms "underground."

2 Roll the acetate sheet into a tube that fits into the can. If the acetate is thin, roll it around several times to make the tube stronger. You should have at least a foot of tube sticking out above the top of the can. Fasten the tube together with clear tape.

3 Set the tube into the can. Pour soil, sand, or gravel in it up to the top of the can. Cover this with the nylon screen or plastic so the worms won't burrow down into the can where you can't see them.

4 When your container is ready, fill it with soil that is moist but not soaking wet. (If you're using a container that can't have drainage holes punched in it, put a layer of sand or gravel at the bottom.) Pack the soil in firmly and fill in all the corners. Leave an inch or so empty at the top.

5 Put an earthworm or two on top of the soil and wait until they dig under. You may want to cover the container or watch carefully in case they try to climb out first. After the worms have burrowed in, cover the container with cheesecloth or screen to let air in and to keep the worms from leaving. This will also keep out insects and other uninvited guests.

6 Since earthworms avoid the light, cover the sides of the container with foil or black paper to keep it dark inside. Put some rotted leaves or other plant material on top of the soil for the worms to eat. Store the container in a cool, dark place and keep the soil moist.

After a while, the worms will probably make some tunnels along the sides of the container. Take the paper off when you want to see the worms and observe what's going on in their burrows. You probably won't get to watch a worm actually making its tunnel, but sometimes you might find it moving up or down through its home, or just resting.

Keep a little notebook or a sheet of paper by the earthworms' house and make a few notes whenever you take a look. Write down the date and the time of day, and then any remarks you have about where the worm is or what it's doing. Or, if you can't see it at all, write that down too. Also mention any special conditions — like a hot spell or a lot of noise — that you think might affect the earthworms' behavior. When you're done, you'll have a record of the earthworms' underground life.

Here are a few suggestions of other things to look for:

1   Do you usually find the worm stretched out or curled up?
2   Does it stay where it is or move out of sight when you remove the dark cover?
3   Do you usually find it at the top or the bottom or somewhere in the middle?
4   If you have more than one worm, do you ever find them in the same burrow?

Investigate the earthworms' eating habits. Put a *small* amount of different kinds of food on the soil under the leaves, and see if it disappears after a few days. Some foods you could try are: coffee grounds, cornmeal, pieces of onion, cabbage, lettuce or other vegetables, bits of fruit, hamburger, or crumbled-up egg. Also offer different kinds of leaves to see if the worms have a favorite.

Find out what effect earthworms' burrowing habits have on the soil. Fill the container with layers of different colored or textured soil.

1 How long does it take for the worms to mix up the layers?
2 Can you figure out why earthworms have been called "nature's plows?"

Remember that no matter how well you care for your worms, or how hard you try to make the "home" just like home, it's not the same as the earthworms' real habitat; and your worms will probably be better off back in the soil where you got them. So, after about a month, let your worms go. Wash out the container and put in new soil. Then, you can always dig up some more worms when you're ready to observe again.

CHAPTER 4

Adaptations: It's What You Do With What You've Got

(Experiments in Earthworm Behavior)

Now that you've examined a few earthworms well enough to get to know them, you can see that they just aren't very well-suited for some kinds of environments. Tunneling through sharp gravel would be pretty rough on them; and they probably wouldn't get much to eat if they had to catch fast-flying insects or crack hard-shelled nuts for food. But on the other hand, a creature with a stiff, hard shell, powerful jaws, agile wings, and keen eyesight probably wouldn't be as successful as the earthworm at living underground and eating leaves.

The worm's long, slender, streamlined body is a perfect shape for moving through the tunnels it makes in the earth that surrounds it. The bristly setae help it to grip the walls as the long and ringed muscles take turns stretching and pulling back, making the worm fatter and thinner, pushing and pulling it along.

Now, of course, there are other ways to move underground. If there weren't, all underground animals would probably look pretty much like earthworms. Moles live underground, for example, and they have legs — special legs, that look like shovels, but legs just the same. Ants live underground. So do sowbugs and sometimes rabbits. All of these have different ways of moving — ways that work quite well for them. But the earthworm's way of moving is very efficient for what it does.

One major task that any animal has to do is to get *energy* by feeding itself. The soil where the earthworm lives is the perfect place to find the dead leaves the earthworm is so highly specialized to eat; and the ability to actually swallow the soil as it tunnels along provides the worm with an extra reserve food supply.

In order to keep eating and getting energy, the worm has to avoid getting eaten itself. Its dark, dirt-like color and *nocturnal* (nighttime) habits help to keep it hidden from predators; and the bristles mean that the lucky bird that does get the worm may have to struggle for it first.

With all its special characteristics, the earthworm is very well adapted to life in the soil. In fact, the

Spiders and sowbugs are among the earthworm's neighbors.

worm's whole body and way of living are geared to survival in its underground world.

In order to survive, all animals, and plants too, must have some special features or adaptations, that equip them to get what they need from their own particular environment.

Adaptations can be almost anything the organism has or does, and they develop in a group of animals — earthworms, for example — by a process called *natural selection*. It works like this: Individuals that have special survival features can pass them on to their young. And the individuals with features that don't help them to survive are more likely not to survive and have young at all. So gradually, most of the individuals in the group wind up with the useful features, while the nonuseful characteristics disappear because there are no more animals that have them.

However, being adapted to an environment is not just a matter of how you're built. It also depends on how you act. Suppose an earthworm that behaves in certain ways has a better chance of getting food or of not being eaten than another earthworm that behaves in different ways. Then the first worm has a better chance of living long enough to pass its special features on to its young; and the second earthworm has a better chance of starving or getting eaten before it has any young at all. After many generations, most of the worms being born would tend to act like the first worm, because they'd inherited these tendencies from their parents. These special ways of behaving, ways that help animals to survive and reproduce in their environment, are called *behavioral adaptations*. The survival features that are built into the animal's body are called *physical adaptations*.

There are many ways an animal could behave toward something in its environment. For example, it could either move away or get closer. Animals tend to live longer if they approach things that are safe and helpful and avoid things that are unpleasant or dangerous. For example, since earthworms live underground and are hardly ever seen up in the sunlight, you might guess that they would be attracted to darkness, and that they would try to get away from light. It seems like a good guess; but just because it makes sense doesn't automatically mean that earthworms really behave that way. It's possible that earthworms come up into the light all the time but get eaten as soon as they poke their heads up. How can we tell if the earthworms are really behaving adaptively, or if it's just some kind of accident that we don't usually see them above ground?

Simply observing earthworms' daily life under ordinary conditions would be the best way to find out what they normally do. But watching earthworms underground is not exactly practical. What we can do is set up an experiment. We can put worms in a situation where they have to make a choice between an area that is dark and one that is lighter; and then we can watch them to see what they do.

Here are two ways to set up the experiment.

What You're Trying to Find Out

How do earthworms react to light and darkness?

METHOD NUMBER 1

What You'll Need (Materials)

- Flat pan (like a sheet-cake pan) or a flat box
- Paper towels
- Cardboard or dark paper
- Water
- Earthworms

What to Do (Procedure)

1 Line the bottom of the pan or box with damp paper towels.
2 Cover one half of the pan with dark paper or cardboard to keep out the light. Leave the other half open.
3 Put a worm right in the middle of the pan or box and watch it for a few minutes. Where does it go first? Where does it stay?

cover to keep out the light   damp paper towel

Do earthworms prefer light or darkness? A simple experiment can help you find out.

4 Write down what happens. A good way to record your results is to make a chart something like this:

Test number	1	2	3	4	5	6	7	8	9
Stays in light area									
Stays in dark area									

When you think your worm has settled on a place to stay, make a check in the right box on the chart.

5 Now take the worm out and repeat the experiment with another worm.

Instead of using just one worm at a time, you could start with five worms on each side of the pan or box and count how many worms are in the light side and how many in the dark side after three minutes.

METHOD NUMBER 2

What You'll Need (Materials)

- Piece of clear acetate (from art supply store)
- Cotton balls
- Dark paper
- Tape
- Earthworms

What to Do (Procedure)

1 Roll the acetate into a tube and tape it together. The tube should be at least as wide as a paper-towel tube and at least a foot long.

2 Cover one half of the tube by wrapping dark paper around it and taping the paper to the tube.

3 Lightly stuff one end of the tube with a cotton ball (so the worm won't leave before the experiment is over).

4 Put a worm in the other end of the tube, and carefully stuff that end with a cotton ball. (Wait until the worm is out of the way so you won't injure it.) Hold the tube level while you put the worm in.

5 Lay the tube on the table or floor, and watch the worm for a few minutes. What does it do? Where does it go?

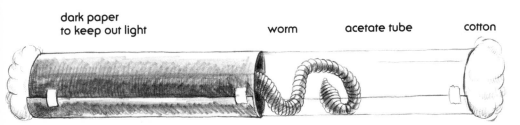

dark paper to keep out light   worm   acetate tube   cotton

Do worms usually move to the light or to the dark part of the tube?

6 Write down your results on a chart like the one shown for method number 1.

7 Repeat the experiment with another worm. If you started the first test by putting the worm in the dark end of the tube, this time put the worm in the light end. Keep changing ends of the tube each time you repeat the experiment.

Suppose some of your worms don't wind up in either the dark area or the light area. What if they just curl up in the middle and don't go anywhere? Or what if they crawl out and escape? Don't worry — just add another line to your chart for keeping track of any unusual behavior.

Are you wondering why you have to repeat the experiment? This is to help make sure that what you saw the first time wasn't just an accident.

Suppose somebody wanted to find out what people from your school do when they get home in the afternoon. Suppose that they came to your house one day and saw you drag yourself slowly into your room, put on your pajamas, crawl into bed, and fall asleep. Suppose they then said, "Aha! People from this school come home in the afternoon, put on their pajamas, and go to sleep at 4 P.M."

It's not hard to figure out that they've made a mistake by coming to see you only once, on a day when you were coming down with the flu. If they visited your house several more times, they might realize that on most days you come racing into the kitchen, gobble up a peanut butter sandwich, and hurry out to meet your friends.

Of course, they still wouldn't know what most people from your school do in the afternoon. Maybe most of the other students do homework for an hour or help with chores before they go outside. These researchers would have to visit several different people on several different days before they could find a more accurate answer to their question.

With earthworms it works the same way. Suppose the first worm you chose was sick? Or so frightened that it acted in a completely unusual way? Maybe you just picked up the rare worm that behaves differently from most others. Even though most earthworms react in similar ways most of the time, you can never be sure just exactly what any particular worm is going to do at any particular time. So you have to do your experiment over and over, with different worms, and you have to keep track of your results. If you count up how many times the worms behave each way, you'll have a better idea of what most worms do most of the time.

If other people are doing these experiments along with you, you can combine all your results on one chart. The more worms you test, the better your chance of finding out how most worms really behave. Also, remember that worms get tired and may stop reacting to anything at all, so don't keep using the same worm over and over.

When you're done, you'll probably find that most worms wind up in the darkened area most of the time. If you don't find this, don't worry. Try to figure out why the worms acted the way they did: was there something about the dark area that made them avoid it? Maybe you'll discover something new! Do the experiments again later on.

Can you figure out how a preference for darkness might help an earthworm to survive? There are at least two hazards that worms can avoid if they stay out of the light. Quite a few animals like to eat earthworms; and if a worm is in the dark, a predator won't be able to see it. Of course, some of the animals that eat earthworms don't need to see them anyway. Plenty of earthworms stay in the dark underground and still get eaten by moles. So staying out of the light doesn't guarantee that a worm won't be eaten; it just helps a little.

Another serious hazard for earthworms is dryness. You noticed before that the worm's skin is very moist. This moisture is necessary for the worm to breathe, because oxygen dissolved in the moisture is taken right in through the earthworm's skin. Obviously, it's very important for the worm not to get dried out; and it's a lot easier for it to stay moist under the damp earth than out in the sunlight. So it seems that staying underground can help an earthworm to survive; and that the worm's automatic reaction — to get away from the light — is a very adaptive way to behave. Our first guess about earthworm behavior turns out to have been pretty good.

But what if the ground itself begins to dry out? If you dig for worms in a place where it's very dry, you'll probably have to dig deeper than someplace where the ground is damp. You might guess that earthworms burrow downward to a moister area and that they avoid drier areas if they can.

Another experiment will help us decide if our guess is right and if earthworms really do adapt to their environment by avoiding dryness. After all, it could well be that the worms do die and disintegrate when the ground gets dry; or maybe they just can't burrow in dry ground. We'll have to test our guess before coming to any conclusions.

Here's one way to test it.

What You're Trying to Find Out

How do earthworms react to damp and dry areas?

What You'll Need (Materials)

- Earthworm
- Paper towels
- Water
- Waterproof surface or a large, flat pan

What to Do (Procedure)

1   Wet a paper towel, wring it out so that it's still damp, and spread it on the table or in one half of a large, flat pan. Next to it spread a dry paper

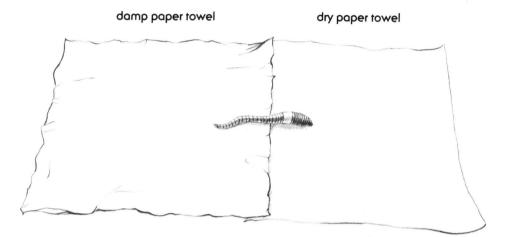

damp paper towel

dry paper towel

Do worms tend to stay on a damp surface or on a dry one?

       towel, with the edges of the two towels overlapping.

2   Put a worm on one of the towels, near the overlapping edges. Watch. What does the worm do? Where does it go? Does it stop on one towel or the other?

3   Write down what happens. Use a chart as you did in the earlier experiment.

Test number	1	2	3	4	5	6	7	8	9
Stays on wet towel									
Stays on dry towel									
Other									

When you think the worm has settled on one towel or the other, make a check on the chart.

4   Take the worm out and repeat the experiment with another worm. If you started with the worm on the damp side the first time, start with the dry side the next time. Change sides each time you start a new test.

Instead of using only one worm, you could start the experiment with five worms on the wet towel and five on the dry towel. Then count how many are on each towel after five minutes.

After you've repeated the experiment at least ten times, take a look at your results. What have you found out? Probably you'll find that most worms will wind up on the damp towel most of the time. This makes sense in terms of earthworm survival, since they die if they get too dried out. If the worm's response to dryness is to get away from it, that probably helps them to stay alive and would be a behavioral adaptation like their response to light. After all, darkness and dampness often occur together under the soil where the earthworm usually stays — a much safer place than in the sunlight and dryness above ground.

Try to make up another experiment to test the worm's response to dry soil instead of to a dry towel. You might fill a container with dry soil on one side and wet soil on the other and see where the worms are after a while. Or put piles of dry and damp soil on the table and see where the worms go. Remember to use more than one worm and to try the experiment several times to be more sure of avoiding accidental behavior. Look in the section called Making Up Your Own Experiments for more help in planning your tests.

In an earlier experiment we investigated the earthworm's response to light when it was given a choice between light and dark areas. The next experiment will look at the earthworm's reactions to light in a different way to find out if the worm notices when light actually shines on it and what parts of the body are most sensitive to light.

What You're Trying To Find Out

How do different parts of the earthworm react to light? How do different colors of light affect the earthworm?

What You'll Need (Materials)

- Earthworm
- Paper towel
- Flashlight
- Dark paper
- Red plastic or cellophane
- Blue plastic or cellophane

What to Do (Procedure)

1 Cover the flashlight with dark paper that has a small hole in it to let light through. Or use a flashlight with a tiny beam of light.
2 Put the worm on a moist paper towel.
3 Darken the room, or use a large box to darken the area around your worm.
4 Aim your beam of light at the worm's tail. Does it react?
5 Slowly move the light toward the head until you've covered the whole length of the worm. Notice how different parts of the worm react. Which parts move most when you shine the light on them and which parts move least?

Which parts of an earthworm are most sensitive to light?

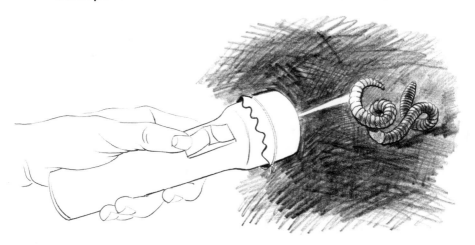

Shine a narrow beam of light on the tail, middle, and head of an earthworm to see which part reacts most vigorously.

6 Make a chart like this to record your results and the results of other people in your class or group. Make a check mark in the square that describes your worm's reaction.

Response	Tail	Middle	Head
No movement			
Slight movement			
Great movement			

7 Repeat the procedure with another worm. (If you use the same worm more than two or three times in a row, it will probably become so tired that it stops reacting altogether.)

8 Now cover the flashlight with red plastic or cellophane before putting the dark paper over it. Try the experiment again, and record your results on another chart.

You'll probably find that *most* worms react to the light by wriggling vigorously; and that this response may be most energetic when the light is aimed at the head of the worm. Does this give you any ideas about where its sensory organs might be concentrated?

You may find that earthworms don't get nearly as excited about red light as they do about white light. In fact, some people find that they can use a red light to hunt for worms at night or to observe the worms' nighttime activities without scaring them away.

Can you think of any possible reasons why earthworms might be less sensitive to red light than to white light? How could their greater sensitivity to white light be an adaptation that helps them to survive? Do you think that reactions to red light would have the same importance?

Try the experiment again with a blue-covered flashlight and see what happens. What would you predict?

Now we know that some parts of the worm may be more sensitive — at least to light — than others. The next experiment will test the earthworm's reactions to another stimulus, touch.

What You're Trying To Find Out

Are earthworms sensitive to touch? How do different parts of the earthworm react to touch?

What You'll Need (Materials)

- Worm
- Paper towel
- Pencil or small stick (optional)

What to Do (Procedure)

1 Put the worm on a moist paper towel.
2 Touch the worm *very gently* on its tail, in the middle, and then on its head. (If you don't want

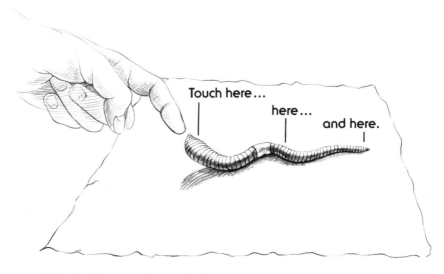

Touch here...

here...

and here.

Touch the worm *gently*. Do some areas seem more sensitive than others?

to touch the worm with your fingers, use a small stick or a pencil. Just remember that a gentle touch is what you need, not a hard poke.)

3   Which parts of the worm move most actively? Least actively?

4   Make a chart again and record your results.

5   Repeat several times with *different* worms.

Which areas of the worm did you find to be most sensitive to touch? Are these the same areas that were sensitive to light? Try to think of an explanation for your findings: how could these areas of sensitivity help the worm survive? Would it be useful or adaptive for the worm to have its middle section be highly sensitive to light or touch?

CHAPTER **5**

⟨⟨⟨⟨⟨⟨⟨⟨⟨⟨⟨⟨⟨⟨⟨⟨⟨⟨⟨⟨⟨⟨⟨⟨

Making up Your Own Experiments

There are probably more things that you'd like to know about earthworms. You might wonder how they react to water, or to different kinds of food, or sounds, or types of soil; what they do if the temperature changes; how fast they can move; or how they grab onto leaves to pull them into a tunnel.

Some questions can be answered by just waiting for a worm to do whatever it is you want to watch. But sometimes you can only find out what you want to know by making up an experiment. You have to set up a special situation so that the worm has a chance to do the particular behavior you're interested in seeing, while you have a chance to see it.

Before you start your experiment, you may have an idea or a guess about what you think will happen. Scientists call such an idea a *hypothesis*. Your results will help you decide if your guess is right or not. Remember that it might not be right. That's the whole purpose of an experiment, to find out one way or the other. The worms may do something entirely different from what you expected — and in that case, you have found out something new. You can then try to figure out why the worms reacted the way they did instead of the way you thought they were going to.

Figure out in advance what materials you need and exactly what you're going to do. Make up a chart or some other handy way of keeping track of your results; and be sure to do a lot of tests.

Try to be sure that your experiment is testing just one thing. For example, if you're interested in the earthworm's reactions to different sounds, be sure to keep the light and temperature the same in all the tests. Suppose that someone wanted to find out what color ice-cream bowl you liked best and gave you a choice between a red one and a blue one. If one bowl had chocolate ice cream and the other had vanilla, how could they tell whether you chose the bowl color or the ice cream flavor? Maybe they could ask you — but remember, you can't ask an earthworm anything!

It's a good idea to write down everything you do. First, because it's very easy to forget exactly what happened; but also because keeping records of observations and experiments is a very important part of scientific investigation. If you've written things down, someone else can come along and try the same experiment and compare their results with yours. If several people get the same results, it's much more likely that those results are correct.

Finally, take a good look at your results and see if you've found the answer to your question; and then try to understand why the worms acted the way they did. Thinking about how the earthworm lives in its normal environment may help you to understand why it does what it does in your experimental environment. Or, it may show that you need to find out more. That's another purpose of experiments — to bring up new questions that haven't been thought of before.

Here is a guide for designing and recording your own experiments:

    I. **Hypothesis.** What did you want to find out? Did you have a guess about what might happen?

    II. **Materials.** What did you use?

    III. **Procedure.** What did you do?

    IV. **Results.** What happened?

    V. **Conclusion.** What answer did you find to your question?

    VI. **Suggestions for further research.** What new questions did this experiment make you think of?

CHAPTER 6

The Earthworm's Insides and Its Life Story

Through your observations and experiments, you have now found out quite a lot about earthworms — mostly just by looking at them. But there may be more things that you'd like to know that you can't easily see — what goes on under the ground, or at night, or inside the worm itself.

To watch worms underground you can build special homes for them, keeping them comfortable while giving yourself a view of many activities that are usually hidden. But much of what happens to an earthworm during its life probably won't happen in your observation house in the same way that it would in the worm's natural environment. And, of course, what is going on inside the worm is even harder to see.

One way of studying how the earthworm is put together is to take it apart — to *dissect* it. But dissection requires special tools and must be done very carefully so that you don't destroy the very parts that you want to see. It also requires specially prepared worms, which are very large and well-preserved. Dissecting a live worm would be very painful to the worm and not very helpful for finding out what's inside anyway. So don't do it. Instead, use another method of research — reading about what other people, with the proper tools and skills, have been able to find out about the earthworm's insides and its life history.

Here's what they've found out. The earthworm, inside and out, is superspecialized for eating and digesting the decayed leaves that are its main source of food. Just as the worm's outside is streamlined for burrowing around in the dirt to find the leaves, its insides are organized to digest them and turn them into energy and building materials for the worm's body.

Imagine the earthworm's body as five long tubes, one inside the other. On the outside is the gooey, slimy stuff that coats the worm, causing its special moist feel. Next are the rings of muscle circling each segment. Inside that are the long strips of muscle going from one segment to another. After the muscles

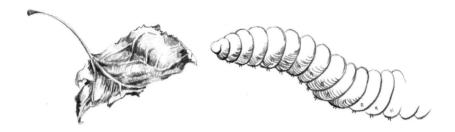

Earthworms eat decayed leaves and other plant parts.

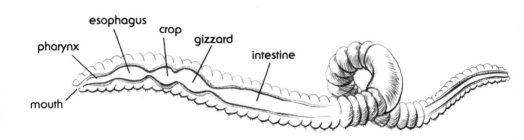

esophagus

crop

gizzard

pharynx

intestine

mouth

Food is digested by juices in the intestine.

Wastes deposited on the ground as *castings* contain many nutrients needed for plant growth.

The earthworm's digestive system is like a factory for turning dead leaves into fertilizer.

comes a hollow space, or *coelom* (sē-lum), filled with fluid; and in the middle is the digestive system.

The coelomic fluid contains special cells that help to get rid of wastes and poisons. It also surrounds and cushions the digestive system, so that the muscles of the digestive tube can keep pushing the food along no matter how the rest of the body may be moving.

Food enters the digestive system at the very front of the worm, through a mouth with a *prehensile* lip, which can grab onto whatever the earthworm is trying to eat. The throat, or *pharynx,* can be pushed forward to help pull leaves into the burrow. Since they have no teeth, earthworms coat the leaves with saliva, which makes them softer and easier to digest. After the food is swallowed, it passes through the *esophagus* to the *crop* and then to the *gizzard* where small stones grind it up before it gets passed on to the *intestine,* which is almost as long as the worm itself. At the end of the intestine is the *anus,* for passing out waste materials.

Nutrients from the food, and the oxygen, taken in through the skin, are carried through the worm's body by blood. There are two main blood vessels, one above and one below the digestive tube. Smaller vessels, including the very tiny *capillaries,* take the blood to all parts of the worm's body, where it delivers food and oxygen and removes wastes. The blood is pumped along by five pairs of "hearts." These are actually enlarged, thick-walled blood vessels connecting the two main blood vessels where they pass the

Five pairs of "hearts"—large, contracting vessels—pump blood all through the earthworm's body.

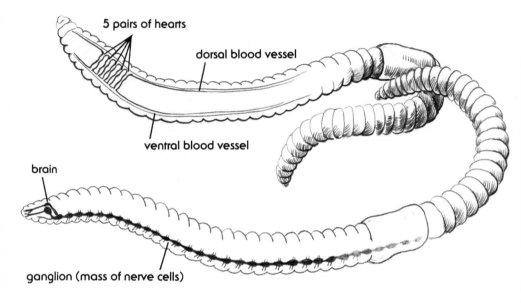

5 pairs of hearts

dorsal blood vessel

ventral blood vessel

brain

ganglion (mass of nerve cells)

Nerve cells receive sensory messages and coordinate movement of the earthworm's muscles.

esophagus. By *contracting*, or squeezing together, the hearts keep the blood flowing through the earthworm's circulatory system.

The earthworm's "brain" is located in the front of its body, along with most of its sensory organs. Nerve cells collect messages and send them all over the worm's body. Although you can't see any of these, you can observe how they make the earthworm react to its surroundings.

This brain doesn't seem to make the earthworm particularly brilliant. But worms do seem to be smart enough to drag leaves into their burrows by the skinniest end first. That would be the easiest way to get them inside, and some people think that worms must be able to to learn this through trial and error, instead of doing it by instinct or by accident. Other experimenters have found that worms could learn to turn toward a comfortable, moist environment and away from a harsh, sandy one or to overcome their aversion to bright light in order to get food.

Each earthworm is both a male and a female and each can produce eggs and fertilize the eggs produced by another worm. During mating, any two adult worms can join together with their heads pointing in opposite directions to fertilize each other's eggs. Then a mucous tube secreted by the clitellum of each worm slips over its head into the soil as an egg case. You might be able to find some of these egg cases in an area where lots of earthworms live. Look for small red or purplish objects about the size of small peas or grains of rice. Or you may find tiny baby worms, which look just like the grown-ups, only smaller and lighter in color.

The eggs usually hatch in about a month, but if the moisture and temperature of the soil are not quite right, the eggs can stay in the case for a year or longer. Even if they freeze or become dried out, the eggs can

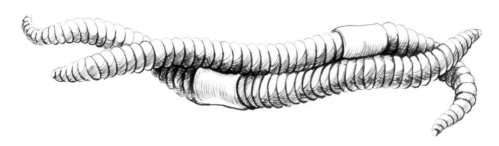

Any two earthworms can mate by joining together and fertilizing each other's eggs.

Later, a tube of mucus secreted by the *clitellum* forms an egg case, which slips off the worm's body.

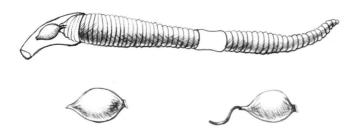

Young worms hatch out into the soil.

hatch out healthy little worms when the conditions are right for them to survive.

Earthworms, like all other animals, must get energy; so they have to eat. While they usually eat decayed leaves, they'll eat a lot of other things as well;

and so they are said to be *omnivorous* — a word that means "eats everything." Of course, that's not completely true — there are plenty of things they won't eat. But when there aren't enough leaves around, earthworms can swallow the soil and digest the little

Earthworms tend to pull leaves into their burrows by the skinniest end first.

bits of plant and animal material that are mixed in with the broken-up rocks and sand. Then they pass the rest right on through their bodies, depositing the waste products on the ground in the shape of tiny pellets called *castings*. The castings are made of soil mixed with digested leaves and chemicals from the worm's body. If you find a lot of these pellets in a patch of soil, there's a good chance you'll find earthworms, too.

Some worms seem to like plugging the openings of their burrows with leaves.

The ability to swallow soil is not only a way to get extra food. It also helps the earthworms in digging their tunnels. If the soil is soft, the worms dig by wedging their front ends into a crack and expanding their bodies to push the soil grains apart. But when the soil is packed hard, they can just eat their way through.

The worm's long, straight or U-shaped burrows may be lined with soft dirt and smooth stones; and

Worms spend the winter curled deep in their burrows.

the openings are sometimes plugged with leaves. At the end of the tunnel may be a chamber where the worm, or several worms, spends the winter rolled up in a ball.

Earthworms spend practically their whole lives in these underground tunnels. Even at night, when they poke their heads out to get leaves, most worms usually keep their tails anchored snugly in the top of the burrow.

Some worms seem to like lying hidden just inside the burrow's opening during the day — making it possible for an alert early bird to grab them.

Being caught by a bird is just one of the many catastrophes that can happen to an earthworm and prevent it from living to a ripe old age. Getting eaten is a major hazard, because many different predators love to eat earthworms. Moles, for example, rely on earthworms for most of their food. They may even bite off a worm's front end and store the body for the winter!

Earthworms can get sick. When they do, they tend to leave their burrows and wander around and die. Some people think that the dead worms you find on the sidewalk after a rain may be these that were already sick.

Humans also can be dangerous to earthworms. Many pesticides and other chemicals are poisonous to them, and of course they may be dug up and used for fish bait. Some get chopped in two by a gardener's shovel, but the worm may survive this catastrophe. If it's lucky enough to be cut at the right spot — before the first twelve segments or after the last four or five — the earthworm has a remarkable ability to *regenerate* or grow new parts. Even though it's limited, such an ability is obviously very useful in helping an individual earthworm keep on living its hazardous life.

As you have discovered, the worm has many other ways of surviving dangers. Being hard to see is one, and staying underground is another. Of course these methods don't always work. But they're successful often enough for many earthworms to live long enough to produce new earthworms. And the new worms, like their parents, come equipped with a host of specialized features to help assure their survival in their very specialized part of the world.

CHAPTER 7

❧❧❧❧❧❧❧❧❧❧❧❧❧❧❧❧

Earthworms in the Soil

An acre of soil may be home to as many as a million earthworms. Wherever they occur — and remember, that's almost everywhere in the world — their activities shape the soil as surely as the demands of life in the soil have influenced the form and function of the worm.

Soil itself is composed of two main parts. The first part is broken-up rocks — clay, sand, and gravel — *eroded* or worn away from larger stones and mountains and carried by wind and water. The second part is decaying *organic* material — the remains of living things. This leftover organic material, or *humus*, is added to the soil when *organisms* die and decay. Humus helps hold water in the soil and keeps the ground from getting too hard for plants to grow. Improving the humus content of the soil is one of the main effects that the earthworm has on its environment.

Earthworms share the soil with ants and many other animals.

The soil isn't just something that lies around under your feet. It is home not only for earthworms but for countless other animals as well. It provides support for plants and supplies them with water and *nutrients* — the nourishing chemicals necessary for growing and for replacing injured and worn-out tissues. And finally, soil is a link in a recycling process that moves vital materials through the bodies of living things and back to the soil again. As it goes along digging, eating, and digesting, the earthworm affects all these soil functions.

Earthworms are truly prodigious diggers and earthmovers. With their habit of swallowing hard soil and their ability to squeeze between and push apart softer soil crumbs, they can move through heavy clays and budge particles that weigh fifty times as

As they tunnel through the soil, earthworms have been known to move small stones 50 times their own weight.

much as they do. Layers of cinders spread over the soil have been totally buried by earthworms' actions, and big rocks have been completely covered up.

All this digging not only moves around a lot of dirt; it also helps make the soil more habitable for many of the other occupants. Turning the soil lets in air, and the worms' tunnels provide spaces for the air and for the water needed by underground animals. Plants need this air and water too; and as the growing roots push through the soil, they often follow the easier pathway of an earthworm's burrow.

Earthworms' burrowing mixes and sifts the soil, breaks up clods of dirt, and buries stones. They carry leaves and other organic matter down and bring nutrients and humus up to the top. You may have observed the earthworm's earth-turning action if you put distinct layers of different colored or different textured soil in your observation container and watched to see how long it took the earthworms' plowing to stir it up into a well-mixed mess.

While the earthworms' travels move the soil around, their eating and digesting actually help form the soil by adding humus and important chemicals and by recycling essential materials. Some people think of the earthworm as a "factory" for producing fertilizer and humus — a sort of streamlined digestive tube that takes in particles of minerals and organic matter and puts out wastes that are rich in humus and in the nutrients essential for plant growth.

The old, decayed leaves and other plant parts that earthworms eat contain many of the chemicals

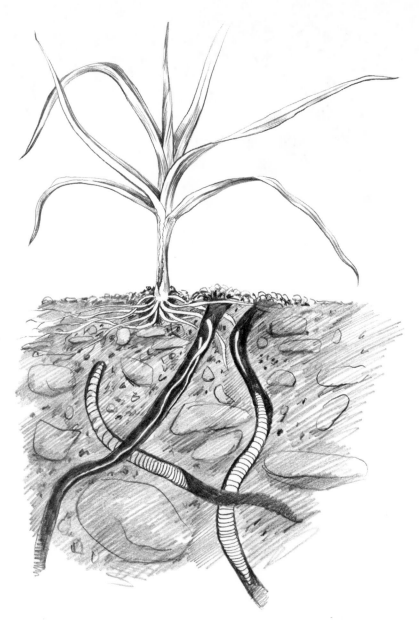

Pushing their way through the soil, growing plant roots
sometimes follow the easier paths of an earthworm's
burrow.

that plants need to live and grow. But these nutrients are locked up in the dead leaves and can't be used by living plants. After being eaten by an earthworm, the rotting plant material is ground up in the crop of the worm and mixed with digestive chemicals and bacteria. The nutrients needed by the worm are absorbed into its body and the leftovers are deposited in the soil as the tiny, pellet-shaped castings. The chemicals that come out of the worm are in different combinations from when they went in; the new forms are ones that can be easily taken from the soil by growing plants. In other words, the worm changes rotten leaves into fertilizer.

We're usually unaware of the thousands of earthworms under our feet. Yet one researcher estimates that earthworms process 40 tons of topsoil per acre in some parts of England, and 200 tons per acre in parts of the Nile Valley. With their mixing, digging, burrowing, fertilizing and humus-making activities, earthworms have an immense impact on the soil — its texture, its fertility, and its ability to support everything that lives in it or on it, especially the plants that form the basis of our own food supply.

To test this impact, people in the U.S. Department of Agriculture tried this experiment about thirty years ago: To one batch of poor soil they added dead worms, fertilizer, and grass seed. To the other, they added live worms and grass seed only — no fertilizer. The soil with the live worms grew four times as much grass as the other! (You might like to try this kind of experiment yourself.)

~~~~~~

CHAPTER 8

Community Relations: Everything Has to Eat Something Else

By now you've discovered quite a bit about how the earthworm is built and how it acts; and you'll probably agree that it's very well-suited, or adapted, to its own special environment. The main feature of that environment is, of course, the soil itself; but it also includes such things as air and water, plants, and other animals.

Together all these parts form a *community*, of which the earthworm is just one member. As they go about their business of trying to survive, all the plants and animals keep running into each other in one way or another. They can't make a living all by themselves, but only through some connection with their neighbors.

Most of these connections have to do with eating or being eaten. That's because every organism has to get food and energy in order to survive; and all organisms, except for green plants, get their food and energy by eating something.

Green plants are different, because they can make their own food, using energy from the sun and chemicals from the air, soil, and water. Green plants are therefore called food *producers,* and their food-making process is *photosynthesis.* Animals can't make their own food this way. They have to get it by eating plants, or by eating other animals that ate plants in the first place; so they are called *consumers.* And finally there are the tiny bacteria and other organisms, called *decomposers,* that digest dead plant and animal material.

One way to think about these "who eats whom" relationships is to trace *food chains.* For example, suppose a clover plant growing in a sunny spot uses the sun's energy to make food, and then is eaten by a rabbit. Then the rabbit is eaten by a fox. The links from clover to rabbit to fox can be called a food chain. Usually nobody eats the fox until it dies, and then some decomposers would be added to the chain. The animals in the chain are sometimes "eaters" (like the rabbit when it eats the clover), and sometimes "eatees" (like the rabbit when it's eaten by the fox). You

A food chain: Energy from the sun is captured by green plants and passed on to other organisms as they eat and get eaten.

can probably think of lots of different food chains yourself.

Naturally the earthworm is involved in food chains too, eating and being eaten just like everybody else. You might draw a food chain from a plant's leaf to an earthworm to a robin; or from a leaf to a worm to a frog to a snake. Or an even longer chain from the leaf to the worm to a fish to a bigger fish to a human.

In fact, earthworms are parts of several different chains: like most animals, they eat and are eaten by more than just one thing. Moles gobble up worms while they're under the ground, and birds grab them as they lie hidden at the mouths of their burrows. Turtles, snakes, and toads eat worms. People use them as bait for catching fish, and in some parts of the world they even find the worms themselves very tasty. And of course, when earthworms die, their bodies get eaten by decomposers — just like the bodies of all the other members of the community.

If you try to draw all the food chains that might include earthworms, you'll have to draw a lot of links connecting the worm to each of its predators; and then from each predator to the other kinds of food it eats; and then to the animals that eat the predators themselves. Pretty soon all those nice, neat, simple food chains you had imagined are all connected to each other, tangled and woven together into a giant, complicated *food web.*

Moving along the food chains in the web are *matter* — the actual physical stuff that the plants and animals are made of — and the *energy* that makes everything move along.

Animals get their energy from food. They use it to move and grow and even to get more energy by finding and eating more food. Energy not used in these ways can be stored in muscles, fat, and other body tissues.

Food chains are connected in a complicated, interwoven tangle called a food web.

When the animal is eaten, this stored energy goes to the eater. But the energy that was spent growing, moving, and eating is not available to the next animal, so at each step in the food chain there's a little less energy available than there was at the step before. Green plants have to keep capturing more energy from the sun to pass along the food chain and to keep everything moving.

On the other hand, there are no new materials to be added. The same matter has to be used and rearranged and used again, over and over and over.

You might imagine these basic materials as chemical building blocks, which can be put together in many different combinations, then broken down into their simplest parts, put back together in other combinations, and recycled again and again.

The building blocks are taken into the bodies of living things from food, water, soil, and air. The organisms use the chemicals to build and operate their bodies. Substances that they can't use are given off as waste products. Then, if the animal or plant is eaten, the materials in them are passed on to the next animal in the food chain. At the "end" of the chain, the original supplies are still around somewhere — either in the last animal's body or out in the environment where they were put as wastes. These wastes and the bodies of dead plants and animals are food for the decomposers.

The decomposers break the materials down into the basic chemical building blocks that we had when we started out — units that can be taken up by the green plants and started through the food chain again.

And that's where the earthworm comes in. Its role in the food chain is not just as a consumer of plant stuff. It also gives an extra little push to the movement of some vital materials through the chain and back to the beginning.

Plant nutrients taken from the environment are returned to it through decomposition when the plants die, or when their leaves drop to the ground and decay. Part of this decomposition happens in the worm's body. By digesting rotted leaves as they do, the worms help get the food materials ready for other decomposing organisms and help to put the nutrients back into the soil where plants can use them. And since plants are such important energy-getters for all other living things, all the participants in the food web benefit from the earthworm's special contribution to the soil.

CHAPTER 9

Earthworms:
Who Needs 'Em?

You can probably see by now that you couldn't really figure out too much about earthworms without thinking about the soil they live in and the rotting leaves that they eat.

Connections and relationships like this are everywhere among the plants and animals and other parts of the environment. Like the earthworms, all kinds of living things have become adapted to their surroundings so that they can get the supplies they need in order to survive. Like earthworms, they all depend on their neighbors in many different ways; and all in some way, however small, have an effect on the environment in which they live. Even those that

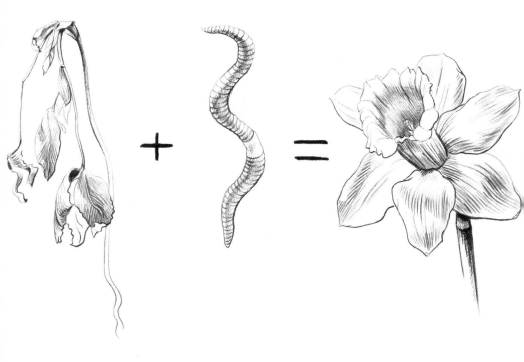

If it weren't for earthworms and other decomposers, all the chemicals necessary for life would be locked up in the bodies of plants and animals—and no new organisms could grow!

are very far apart from each other are connected — by the far-reaching links in food chains and food webs and by participation in the never-ending cycles that use and reuse the limited supply of materials available on earth.

Understanding these connections between living things and their environment is very important for people because we too are part of this network.

Whether we like it or not, we too depend on other animals and plants; and we too influence and change our surroundings with our activities. And whether we like it or not, changes in any part of our environment will have some effect on us, even though the changes may seem very small, or very far away, or very unimportant. After all, even such unlikely prospects as earthworms have turned out to be rather significant creatures. Just imagine how different our planet would be if they weren't around to share it with us.

Glossary

acidic   having characteristics of acids, such as a sour taste.

adaptation   any characteristic that helps an organism survive in its environment.

annelid   worm with a body made of joined segments, or rings.

anus   opening at end of digestive system, through which waste is excreted.

behavioral adaptation   characteristic behavior or way of acting that improves an organism's chances of survival.

capillaries   tiny blood vessels in which nutrients and wastes are exchanged.

casting   waste products of earthworm digestion.

clitellum   a swollen ring around earthworm's body. The clitellum secretes mucus necessary for fertilization and for the egg cases that protect the developing embryos.

community   a group of animals and plants living together and interacting in the same environment.

consumers   organisms that obtain energy by eating other living things.

contract   to squeeze together or shrink.

coelom   body cavity; a fluid-filled space between the earthworm's body wall and digestive system.

crop   thin-walled sac just behind the earthworm's esophagus where food is stored briefly on its way through the digestive system.

decomposers   organisms that digest and break down into simpler chemicals the wastes and dead bodies of other plants and animals.

decomposition   process in which substances are taken apart or broken down into simpler chemical parts.

dissect   to cut apart or separate for detailed examination.

energy   the ability to do work by moving matter; the capacity to make things move, grow, or change.

erode   to wear away or disintegrate.

esophagus   the food canal that leads from the mouth to the crop and gizzard.

food chain   transfer of food energy through producers, consumers, and decomposers.

food web   a complex, interlocking series of food chains.

gizzard   sac behind the earthworm's crop. The gizzard has heavy muscular walls that grind up food with the help of small stones swallowed by the worm.

habitat   place or environment where a plant or animal naturally lives, grows, finds food and shelter, and raises its young.

humus   mixture of decaying organic matter and inorganic compounds in soil; major source of plant nutrients.

hypothesis an unproved idea that might explain certain facts; used as a basis for further investigation.

interpret to explain the meaning of something; to make it understandable.

intestine long tube at end of digestive system; location of final digestion of food and absorption of nutrients.

matter anything that has weight and takes up space.

natural selection process in which individual organisms that are better adapted to a particular environment live longer and have a better chance of leaving more offspring than individuals that are less well adapted. As time goes on, the population will include a greater percentage of individuals that have inherited favorable characteristics from their parents.

nocturnal active during the night.

nutrient substance needed for normal growth and development of an organism.

observe to pay special attention to something; to notice or perceive it; to examine carefully.

omnivorous able to use both plants and animals as food sources.

organic having to do with or being derived from living organisms.

organism any living thing.

pharynx throat.

photosynthesis process in which green plants, exposed to the energy of sunlight, combine water and carbon dioxide to produce oxygen and basic food substances.

physical adaptation physical characteristics that improve an organisms chances of survival.

predators animals that live by killing and eating other animals.

prehensile adapted for siezing or grasping.

producers organisms that change energy from the sun into food energy, which can be used by consumers. By making their own food, green plants directly or indirectly produce almost all the world's food energy.

recycle to use again and again.

regenerate to grow a new part as a replacement for one that's been hurt or lost.

segment section or part.

seta a short, stiff hair or bristle. The four pairs of setae on each segment of an earthworm help it to move through the ground.

Further Reading

Allen, Dorothy Holmes, and the editors of Country Beautiful. *The Story of Soil*. New York: G.P. Putnam's Sons, in association with Country Beautiful Corporation, 1971.

Cromer, Richard. *Soil*. Chicago: Follett Publishing Co., 1967.

Darling, Lois. *Worms*. New York: William Morrow & Co., 1972.

Hess, Lilo. *The Amazing Earthworm*. New York: Charles Scribner's Sons, 1979.

Keen, Martin L. *The World Beneath Our Feet*. New York: Julian Messner, 1974.

Lauber, Patricia. *Earthworms, Underground Farmers*. Champaign, Il.: Garrard Publishing Co., 1976.

Nespojohn, Katherine V. *Worms*. New York: Franklin Watts, Inc., 1972.

Rhine, Richard. *Life in a Bucketful of Soil.* New York: Lothrop, Lee & Shepard Books, 1972.

Simon, Seymour. *Discovering What Earthworms Do.* New York: McGraw-Hill Book Co., 1969.

Simon, Seymour. *Beneath Your Feet.* New York: Walker & Co., 1977.

White, William. *An Earthworm is Born.* New York: Sterling Publishing Co., 1975.

■ These books are a little more difficult:

Buchsbaum, Ralph Morris. *Animals Without Backbones: An Introduction to the Invertebrates* 3rd rev. ed. Chicago: University of Chicago Press, 1976.

Darwin, Charles. *The Formation of Vegetable Mould Through the Action of Worms.* (First published in 1881.) *In* Howard, Albert, intr. *Darwin on Humus and the Earthworm.* London: Faber and Faber, 1966.

Farb, Peter. *Living Earth.* New York: Harper Colophon Books, Harper & Row, Publishers, Inc. 1959.

Schaller, Friedrich. *Soil Animals.* Ann Arbor: University of Michigan Press, 1968.

■ Some ideas for experiments and activities in this book came from:

Katagiri, George, et al. *Ecology.* Self-Paced Investigations for Elementary Science (SPIES). Morristown, N.J.: Silver Burdett Co., 1976.

Elementary Science Study (ESS). *Teacher's Guide for Earthworms* Nashua, N.H.: Delta Education, 1971, 1969.

Index

S

Segment, 14, 61, 81
Sensory organs, 54–55
Setae, 15, 19, 81
Soil, 62–67
Survival, 60–61

T

Throat, 53
Touch, sensitivity to, 45–46